Solid, Liquid, or Gas?

IT'S SCIENCE!

Solid, Liquid, or Gas?

Sally Hewitt

CHILDREN'S PRESS®

A Division of Scholastic Inc.

NEW YORK • TORONTO • LONDON • AUCKLAND • SYDNEY
MEXICO CITY • NEW DELHI • HONG KONG
DANBURY, CONNECTICUT

This edition published in 2007 by Franklin Watts
338 Euston Rd
London NW1 3BH

Franklin Watts Australia
Level 17/207 Kent St
Sydney NSW 2000

Series editor: Rachel Cooke
Art director: Robert Walster
Designer: Mo Choy
Picture research: Susan Mennell
Photography: Ray Moller unless otherwise acknowledged
Consultant: Sally Nankivell-Aston
Copyright © Franklin Watts 1997

A CIP catalogue record for this book
is available from the British Library.
ISBN 978 0 7496 7771 8

Dewey Classification 530.4

Printed in Malaysia

Photographic acknowledgements:
Robert Harding pp. 10r, 19t, 26tl
John and Penny Hubley p. 17tr
Image Bank p. 6r, 13br, 24br
Magnum Photos p. 27tl (Steve McCurry)
Oxford Scientific Films p. 26br (Breck P. Kent/Earth Scenes)
Tony Stone pp. 26tr (Charles Krebs), 27tr (David Woodfall); Zefa p. 11bl
The publishers would also like to thank Tridias, 6 Bennett Street, Bath BA1 2QP 01225 314730 for their help with
some of the items featured on the title page and pp. 7, 14, 25 and 29.
Thank you, too, to our models: Claire Sutcliffe. Henry Cheese-Probert and Jordan Morris-Hudson
Franklin Watts is a division of Hachette Children's Books, an Hachette Livre UK company.

Contents

Useful Materials

The things we use and see around us are made of all kinds of different **materials**.

Bricks, metal, and glass are all materials that are good for building. They are all **solids**.

Can you spot bricks, metal, and glass in this building? How has each one been used?

Cardboard, string, plastic, and cotton balls are not good for making real buildings. But they are very useful materials. Why are they useful? The pictures will give you some ideas.

 **THINK ABOUT IT!**

What might happen if you built a real house out of cotton balls, string, and cardboard?

 TRY IT OUT!

Look at some of the things around you, such as a carpet, a door, or a spoon. Feel them as well.
Do you know what materials they are made from?

Pouring

Oil, liquid soap, honey, and water are different kinds of **liquid**. Liquids can be poured.

 **TRY IT OUT!**

Find four bowls and try pouring oil, liquid soap, honey, and water into them. Which one pours very slowly? What happens to the liquid in the bowl?

THINK ABOUT IT!

Why do you think we usually keep liquids in containers? What other liquids can you think of?

Liquid does not have a **shape** of its own. Look what happens when the same amount of water is poured into these different shaped containers.

The water fills up the space and becomes the same shape as the container.

Salt and flour are not liquids but they can be poured because they are made up of thousands of tiny grains.

THINK ABOUT IT!

You can pour salt into a pile. Can you pour water into a pile too?

9

Gas

Did you know that **air** is a kind of **gas**? We can't see it, but it is all around us.

You breathe air in and out of your lungs.

 TRY IT OUT!

Blow into a balloon. You can see the air you breathe filling out the balloon. Let the air escape and feel it rushing out of the balloon.

This balloon is filled with a kind of gas called helium. Helium is lighter than air, so the balloon **floats** upwards.

Hot air is lighter than cold air so a hot air balloon floats upwards, too.

A car engine burns **fuel** and gives off a kind of gas called exhaust.

A burning fire gives off a kind of gas called smoke.

At first, you can see smoke and exhaust, then they mix into the air and you can't see them any more.

We burn natural gas for cooking and keeping warm.

Water

Water is a very important liquid. We need to drink water to stay healthy and to wash in it to keep clean.

Plants need water to grow.

💡 **THINK ABOUT IT!**

Why do boats need water?
Why do firefighters need water?
What other ways do we use water?

Water is not always a liquid.
When it is cooled and **freezes,**
it becomes ice. Ice is a solid.

When water is heated up it becomes
steam. Steam is a gas.

👁 LOOK AGAIN

Find some solid materials on page 6.
Find some liquids on page 8.
Find some gases on pages 10 and 11.

An iceberg is a gigantic block of frozen water.
When the sun warms it, the ice **melts** back
into water and mixes with the sea.

Water Test

Some things will float and some will **sink** when you put them in water.

The duck floats and so do all these other objects.

Marbles, a spoon, and a pebble sink.

Look at the different objects on this page. Do you think they are heavy or light? Do you know what they are made of?

TRY IT OUT!

Collect some objects.
Guess whether the objects will float or sink.
Put them in a bowl of water to see if you were right.

When you put some materials in water, they soak up the water and feel soggy.

Other materials don't soak up water at all. They are **waterproof**.

TRY IT OUT!

Find a piece of paper, a piece of plastic, a sponge, and some wool. Feel them. Then guess what will happen when you put them in the water. Which ones will soak up water? Try it out to see if you were right.

Melting

Butter, chocolate, and a wax candle are all solid.

When they are heated, they melt and become liquid.

They become solid again when they cool down.

 **TRY IT OUT!**

Ask an adult to help you melt some chocolate in a bowl over a saucepan of simmering water. Pour the melted chocolate into pastry cutters. When the chocolate cools, it will set into new shapes.

Plastic melts and becomes soft and runny when it is heated.

Melted plastic can be poured into a **mold**. When it cools down, it sets into a the shape of the mold.

Look around you to find some things like these that are made of molded plastic.

Metal melts when it is heated to a very high temperature. Molten metal was poured into a mold to make this toy truck.

Changing Shape

Clay is a kind of mud.
You can squash, press, and roll
it into new shapes.

When clay is fired in a **kiln**, it dries out
and becomes hard. You can't
change the shape of a fired pot –
unless you smash it!

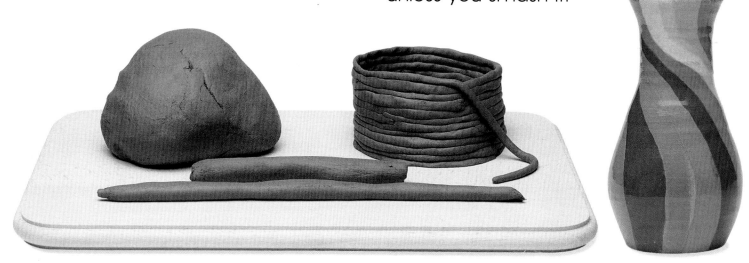

Pastry dough is soft and can be
made into new shapes.
When pastry dough is cooked, it
hardens and becomes good to eat!

👁 LOOK AGAIN

Look again at page 17.
What happens to metal and plastic when they are heated?

Thin sheets of metal can be cut, hammered, and pressed into new shapes.

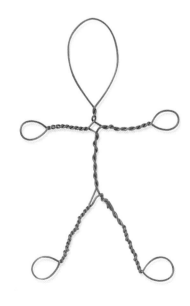

You can curl, twist, and bend wire. It is good for making models because it will stay in its new shape.

💡 **THINK ABOUT IT!**

What else could you use wire for?

Dissolving

If you look at salt and sugar through a magnifying glass, you will see hundreds of tiny **crystals**.

Salt and sugar crystals **dissolve** when they are mixed with water and make a **solution**.

 TRY IT OUT!

Mix a spoonful of sugar in 4 ounces of warm water. Keep stirring until the sugar disappears.

Dip your finger in the solution you have made and taste it. You can't see the sugar but you can taste it; it is still there.

Look what happens when you mix cooking oil with water. It breaks up. But it will not dissolve however hard you stir.

TRY IT OUT!

Mix a spoonful each of instant coffee, tea leaves, and jam in separate cups of warm water. Do any of them seem to "disappear" like sugar? What happens to the color of the water? Which one will not dissolve?

Paper

Did you know that paper is made from tiny pieces of wood mixed with water to make wood **pulp**?

The pulp is squeezed out and rolled into sheets of paper.

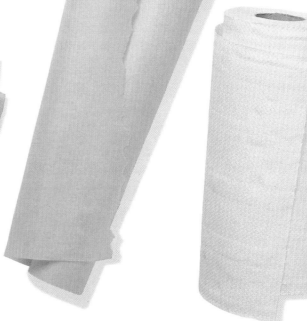

 TRY IT OUT!

Collect different kinds of paper like these. Feel them. Try writing on them, tearing, folding, and cutting them.
Which one is best for cutting?
Which ones tear easily?

Which paper on the opposite page would you use to write a letter?

Which paper would you use to wrap a present?

Which paper would be good for mopping up?

Which paper could you use to wrap sandwiches?

 THINK ABOUT IT!

Paper is used in hundreds of different ways.
How many ways of using paper can you think of?

What Material?

Do you know what this dining room chair, the baby's bowl and mug, the saucepan, and the window panes are made of?

Can you think why they are made of each type of material?
Look at the opposite page to help you work out the answers.

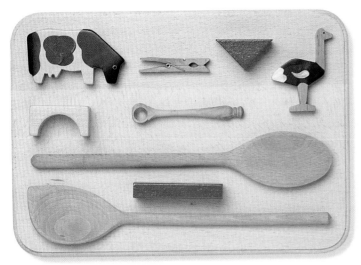

Wood can be cut and carved.
It is strong but it burns easily.

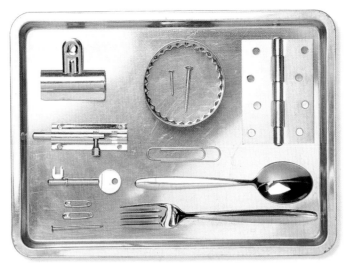

Metal is strong and does not
burn easily.

Plastic is tough and light. It can be
molded into different shapes.

You can see through glass,
and it breaks easily.

 THINK ABOUT IT!

Glass would not be a good material for making a mug for a baby.
Why not? Could a saucepan be made of wood?

Natural or Man-Made?

Some of the materials we use are **natural**.
They come from animals, plants, and from the ground.

Wool comes from a sheep's soft coat.

Wood comes from trees, the
biggest plants of all.

Marble is a kind of rock.

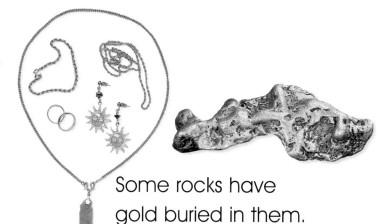

Some rocks have
gold buried in them.

👁 LOOK AGAIN

Look again at page 18 to find another natural material.

Natural materials can be used to make different kinds of materials.

Oil from deep under the ground is used to make material called nylon.

Sand is one of the materials used to make glass.

LOOK AGAIN

Look again at page 22 to find another **man-made** material.

Useful Words

Air Air is a kind of gas. We can't see it but it is all around us. People, animals, and plants all need air to live.

Crystals Some solids are made up of flat-sided shapes called crystals. Tiny grains of sugar and salt are crystals.

Dissolve When a solid mixes in with water and seems to disappear, we say it dissolves.

Float Boats float on water. Balloons can float in air. They do not sink under the water or down to the ground.

Freeze When water is cooled and turns into ice, we say it freezes.

Fuel Fuel, such as oil, is something we burn to make energy.

Gas The air around us is a kind of gas, so is steam from boiling water. A gas does not have a shape of its own.

Kiln A kiln is a type of oven where clay pots are dried out, or fired, at very high temperatures.

Liquid Water, milk, and oil are all kinds of liquid. Liquid can be poured and it does not have a shape of its own.

Man-Made Some materials we use, such as plastic and paper, are made by people. We call them man-made materials.

Materials Wood, glass, and paper are all different materials. Materials are what things are made of.

Melt When a solid is heated and turns into a liquid, we say it melts.

Mold A mold is a hollow shape which is used to give its shape to something, such as plastic.

Natural A plant, an insect, and a rock have not been made by people. They are all natural.

Pulp Pulp is a slushy mixture of tiny pieces of wood and water used to make paper.

Shape Every solid object has it own shape. A pencil is a long, thin shape and a ball is a round shape.

Sink Some things, such as a rock or a coin, will not float on water. They sink down into it.

Solid Solid things are neither liquid nor gas. They have shape of their own.

Solution When some crystals, such as sugar and salt, are mixed with water, they dissolve and make a solution.

Waterproof Some materials are waterproof. When they are put in water, they do not soak it up at all.

Index

About This Book

Children are natural scientists. They learn by touching and feeling, noticing, asking questions, and trying things out for themselves. The books in the *It's Science!* series are designed for the way children learn. Familiar objects are used as starting points for further learning. *Solid, Liquid, or Gas?* starts with building bricks and explores materials.

Each double page spread introduces a new topic, such as liquids. Information is given, questions asked, and activities suggested that encourage children to make discoveries and develop new ideas for themselves.
Look out for these panels throughout the book:

TRY IT OUT! indicates a simple activity, using safe, materials, that proves or explores a point.
THINK ABOUT IT! indicates a question inspired by the information on the page but which points the reader to areas not covered by the book.
LOOK AGAIN introduces a cross-referencing activity which links themes and facts through the book.

Encourage children not to take the familiar world for granted. Point things out, ask questions, and enjoy making scientific discoveries together.